"For a star to be born,
There is one thing that must happen:
A gaseous nebula must collapse.

So collapse.
Crumble.
This is not your destruction.

This is your birth"

- n.t.

the future seemed fragile
the smallest change and everything would shatter
but shattering became calming
and fragility became strength

The thoughts that used to crowd my vision seem small,
Microscopic
Compared to the fragments of broken dreams tearing
me apart
The problems that seem insignificant plunge the knife
deeper
Until it begins to bleed out the letters that form suffering,
Suffering in plain sight.
Why is it when the thoughts begin
We feel everything over again.
I've felt lost for so long
Trying to find my way home,
Dying since i got here,
Forgetting to enjoy the view.
I ask myself,
Would the person I used to be, be proud of me now?

You long for me
Coming back more powerful every time.
Crushing the empty thoughts as you pass,
Weakening my fragile structure
Making it harder to breathe.
I never fail to welcome you home
But your return destroys a new spark of confidence
growing within,
Your return makes me question my sanity,
Makes me feel angry towards uncontrollable feelings.

The beautiful sunrise that calms your storms is fighting
her own silent battle
But inside the waves that crash against her dreams
Begin to seep through the cracks in her facade,
Made so carefully over the years.
The beautiful sunrise becomes a hurricane
And her once glowing eyes become a pool of
emptiness.
A shell of what was.

Who are you when the storm begins and the rain pours
down your spine?

The only one who sees this side of me is the twisted image in the mirror.
So unfamiliar,
So broken.

Life opened its arms and embraced me in its empty
canvas
Watching me grow and paint my own story
Only to let go and stare as it allowed me to fall to the
ground
Shattering into so many pieces.

And she embraced the chaos when her life began to
align
And the tears began to dry.

As the sun set with you,
It rose with her.
You're the one in my life that makes the days seem a
little brighter
And the deep feelings a little less hurtful.
You are my sunshine,
From you they are born.
The
Words
Of
The
Sun.

One day i'll be the brightest star
But until that day
I will shine behind the clouds,
Not because im afraid
But because I've still got a long way to go.

Recently i've felt like stars on a cloudy night
But you blew the clouds out of the way,
To make room for me,
Forgetting the backlash,
Leaving you in the dark.
Don't worry
You won't be there long,
For I will bring you out and allow you to shine brighter
than the rest.

Out of all the perfect flames,
I still choose you.

She is made of poetry, sunlight and patience.

When she made contact with heaven,
She remembered how to fly.

But my darling,
Even Rome fell apart.

I've found myself carrying the weight of the world,
Tangling my mind in tight arms,
Strengthening its grip.
It's time I let myself go and allow my lungs to expand.

If i'm asleep in this world,
Be certain I'm awake in the other.

Even the stars stop and watch,
Admiring your shine.

Can you grasp how rare and beautiful it is that we are
destined to be alive at the exact same time.

She wore pain like a coat,
Personifying insomnia.

And almost instantly i felt drained,
As if all the life had been pulled out of me,
Strand by strand,
Until all that is left is an empty vessel.

You'll never leave my mind.
Like the land and the ocean,
We will always be under the same sky.

The brittle bones that once held me together crumble at the root of the tree.

Think of me when your socks are soaked through and the sky's tears trace your face.

She kept looking where the light filters in for a spark of
hope.

She wore a thousand personalities
Until her real one seeped through and saw the sun.

Perhaps what made her beautiful
Was not her appearance
But that she chose love
When the world was full of hatred
And let the light run wild in the depths of darkness.

My heart pounds at my ribs
And insomnia consumes my dreams.
Drowning in life consuming despondency.

I found myself getting lost within the ocean in your eyes
And the depth within your smile.

I
Spend
Too
Much
Time
Dying
In
My
Own
Head
Wondering
If
Im
Ever
Alive
In
Yours.

She was the personification of rain,
Falling ever so beautifully.

The first time i saw you,
Your eyes glistened
And i knew,
Then,
That we would make something beautiful.

I wonder how long this indestructible silence will cloud
your words,
Blinding my view
Like fog on a bathroom window which cries at the winds
of agony.

One day i will love myself
And on that day,
The clouds will part
And the sunlights touch will stroke my skin
With such delicacy for fear of breaking my once fragile
structure.

Paranoia isn't just being scared of the unknown,
It when your thoughts eat you from the inside out until
you're on the floor screaming for freedom from your own
mind.

The nights I lay sleepless are when I pray for your embrace the most.

Would you still love me if all i could give you was bone
instead of skin.

I don't know the meaning of life
But kissing you
While cold in the winter
Is close enough.

My loneliness blossoms in the rain
For nature has the power to make everything beautiful.

I wish you could see your worth because to me,
You're perfect.

Our relationship is ethereal
We met because our stardust aligned.
Can you grasp the beauty of that single moment,
Changing our lives forever.

The tragic truth is, no one will ever fully understand
these words but me,
No rhyme or phrase will ever make sense of the mess
that consumes something so beautifully poetic.

Sometimes i feel so small,
But so are the stars from here,
That's the paradox of life.

Your mind was shattered,
Fragmented into insignificant pieces,
But you healed:
You filled the cracks with a type of love that has the
power to radiate contentment
And you blocked out the black nights with the sunlight
stored in your heart.
Using benevolence as glue,
You fixed yourself,
You my darling are a work of art.

My structure is brittle
And my mind is scattered
Yet you still see the sunlight in my heart.

Perhaps i'm waiting for something that never going to come,
Like the sun waiting to shine during an eclipse.

Often i feel like i'm chasing happiness
To keep up with life,
But perhaps true happiness only comes when you
realise life is not a race
But a peaceful drive.

Everyone is watching me
And i'm stuck in a glass room
Ready for observation.

Sometimes it feels like the little people that mutter in my mind are smashing rocks against the edge of my brain.

On her bedroom floor she was raw,
Each bone rooting her to the ground,
Growing a forest around my delicate body
Exposing her to the brutality of her mind,
A beautiful ocean of butterflies.

She is a flower
but she isn't gentle,
Every inch of her body
Covered with unique butterflies
Burning with each flutter of the wings,
She longs for acceptance
But fails to accept herself.
Her mirror screaming with each tear that falls
Crying at the sight of her beaten physique.
Despite the mess of life,
When everything dwindles,
She will fall in love with herself again.

Control the fierce parade that marches on your tender
skin,
The sharp wounds that deflate our face,
Wincing and screaming at the busy sun and rain.
Control the soldiers that destroy every ounce of joy,
Leaving you weak to collect yesterday's pieces.
Control it.

Do you even notice there is a storm in my mind or are
you too oblivious to care?

You make me feel alive by sucking the soul out of my
body,
Killing me with every breath.

I struggle to find a word to describe this feeling so for now I'll settle for numb.

Laying with you is like laying under a sky full of stars
Every breath you take adds sparkle to your eyes,
A sparkle brighter than any in the sky.
A love like ours,
Stronger than the forces keeping us on the ground,
A love forbidden in 72 different states
But love that comes from sweet smiles
And soft lips
Shines an intoxicating sense of freedom that love is
eternal.

Just breathe they say as you let out a sigh with every
breath,
A sigh so big it pushes the boats across the ocean
And rustles the leaves in your garden.

Just smile they say as you lay hopeless on the grass,
So hopeless that even a laugh uses every muscle in
your body,
Draining you more and more.

Just eat they say as your physique screams at you
through your mirror,
A scream so loud that the birds stop chirping and the
worms stop burrowing.

Just breathe.
Just smile.
Just eat.

Only the sun, the moon and the stars know the darkest side of me.
They are the storms that create the silence.

For many, sleep is second nature,
An unthinkable task that consumes the body for 7 hours
everyday.

Fro me, sleep is like walking through reality,
Drifting in and out of all sense.
My mind creates the pictures that appear the next day,
Like a perfectly planned slideshow,
Scanning through every moment as if it's raw and
untouched.

Sleep gives me the ability to step into god's library,
I'm free to flick through the future to find tomorrow.
I can find the exact moment that you find love,
I can see the holding of hands under a solid table.

But all good things have a dark side,
Flicking through moment of tomorrow
I get pulled into the act of foreshadowing.
I'm forced to watch as he leaves you:
Breaking away.
I'm made to witness the moment you decide you're not
good enough,
The moment you give up.

I have a gift,
My gift,
Is sleep.

Life is so precious,
Taken and given in seconds.
As day turns to night,
Young turns to old,
Love blossoms into prosperity.

My head is heavy,
Like every thought is weighted,
Adding pressure to my spine.
Slowly making me smaller
Until i eventually give in to the weights
And crumble under the force.

I'm surrounded in an empty room.
The silence,
The thoughts
Pushing in on me.
Crowding my mind.
Peace is a trophy
Won with patience,
Patience with yourself.

Lost in your eyes
I felt myself drift away from reality,
Into a world of our own.
A world of purity and contentment.
But no such world exists,
For we are all fatal flaws in our own stories.

<u>**A few words from the author:**</u>

Thank you for choosing my book! I'm only 16, so having this opportunity is an amazing experience, I hope to continue my writing career for years to come and release more books like this one.

Thank you to my family, my school and my year 10 english teacher for helping me and supporting me to get to this point. It's quite surreal. I'd like to give a special thank you to my amazing girlfriend for reading and giving me feedback on almost every one of my poems as most of them are about her or our relationship.

Thank you for reading my work - keep fighting, keep smiling and keep loving, the best is yet to come.

Contact: sunlightwords16@gmail.com
Instagram: @sunlightwords @iizelle

978-1-71673-136-5

Imprint: Lulu.com

www.ingramcontent.com/pod-product-compliance
Lightning Source LLC
Chambersburg PA
CBHW051230250726
48655CB00006B/2697